How to Win at
CASINO
GAMES

Belinda Levez

TEACH YOURSELF BOOKS

S0-AUJ-079

Long-renowned as the authoritative source for self-guided learning – with more than 30 million copies sold worldwide – the *Teach Yourself* series includes over 200 titles in the fields of languages, crafts, hobbies, sports, and other leisure activities.

Library of Congress Catalog Card Number: 96-72623

First published in UK 1997 by Hodder Headline Plc, 338 Euston Road, London NW1 3BH

A catalogue entry for this title is available from the British Library.

First published in US 1997 by NTC Publishing Group
An imprint of NTC/Contemporary Publishing Company
4255 West Touhy Avenue, Lincolnwood (Chicago), Illinois 60646 – 1975 U.S.A.

Typeset by Transet Limited, Coventry, England.
Printed in England by Cox & Wyman Ltd, Reading, Berkshire.

Impression number	10	9	8	7	6	5	4	3	2
Year			2000	1999	1998	1997			

795
LEV
2/98

CONTENTS

INTRODUCTION

Many people gamble in casinos with varying degrees of success. Some win money but a lot lose. Many of the losses could be avoided. They are often due to a lack of knowledge about the games and poor methods of play. Too many people rely on luck instead of skill.

Some games are simply not worth playing because they give poor returns to the player. Others which give a fairer chance may incorporate some bets that are not worth bothering with.

This book aims to teach you how profitable the various games are so that you can make an informed choice about those that are worth playing. The rules are also described so that you can learn how to play properly. You will be taught how to get better value for money, as well as the methods of play which maximise winnings whilst keeping losses to a minimum. Many illustrated examples are given to make the understanding of the games easier.

The issues that you need to consider when gambling are covered, along with advice on where to gamble. The dangers involved with playing in illegal casinos are highlighted, and you are also shown how to avoid the tricks used by casinos to make you spend more money.

By the end of the book you should be a more informed gambler with a better understanding of the subject. With plenty of practice you should also become a more skilful player and – hopefully – a winner instead of a loser. Good luck!

1
CASINO GAMBLING

A fair chance

Whatever game you choose to play, one of the most important considerations is that you have a fair chance of winning. The best way to guarantee this is to gamble only in legal establishments.

Although illegal casinos and private games may offer some concessions which appear to work in the player's favour, such as tax-free betting and better payout odds, it is far too easy for the house to cheat. There are lots of ways in which gamblers can be duped.

Card games are particularly vulnerable to cheating. With poker, knowing what cards the other players are holding can virtually guarantee a gambler's chances of winning. This can be achieved by marking the cards in such a way that they can be read. Small alterations are made to the designs on the backs of the cards. A line may be thickened, dots added or areas shaded. In Figure 1.1, two of the circles on card (b) have been shaded. It is also possible to mark cards in such a way that they are virtually impossible to detect.

There are lots of scams which can be used when the cards are dealt. With practice, a technician (someone skilled at using slight of hand to cheat when the cards are dealt) can deal from the bottom of the pack, deal the second card so that the top card is saved for himself or covertly look at the cards as they are dealt.

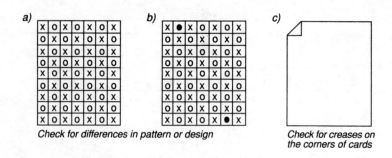

Check for differences in pattern or design

Check for creases on the corners of cards

Figure 1.1 Cheating using marked cards

By creating a distraction a cold deck can be substituted for the one in play. A cold deck is a pack of cards arranged in a preset order. A player knowing the order of the cards can ensure that he wins.

Dice can be tampered with in several ways to ensure that they land in the desired manner. Using loaded dice is common. Here, weights are inserted into the dice to ensure that they always fall on to the heaviest side. By filing the edges a cheat can also make them land on his chosen numbers. The numbers on the dice can also be altered to make some scores easier or more difficult to throw.

Roulette can also be fixed. Small needles, invisible to the naked eye, can be inserted into the slots as the wheel is spinning to stop the ball from landing in numbers that are heavily backed.

As well as cheating, illegal casinos may offer you unlimited credit. This can make it very easy for you to go over budget. An illegal casino's methods for recouping the money you owe may also be highly suspect.

Playing in a legal casino is by far the safest way to gamble as you can guarantee that the game will be operated fairly. The casino's procedures make it difficult to cheat. The dealer has no interest in the game, so can be trusted, and you will also be supplied with written rules on request. New packs of cards are used each day and are scrutinised for any marks before use. The shoes (the boxes where cards are placed for dealing) are chained to the tables so that they cannot be substituted for cold decks, and regular checks are made on the dice in play to ensure that they have not been switched for loaded ones.

Casinos

British casinos

Great Britain has over 120 legal casinos. They tend to be found in large towns and cities and in tourist areas. There are over 20 in London. They are strictly controlled by the Gaming Board who issue licences for premises and casino staff. Checks are carried out to ensure that no gaming personnel or casino owners have criminal records. Games played include roulette, blackjack and punto banco. Daily opening hours are from 2.00pm to 4.00am.

United States casinos

Gaming is legal in most of the United States (only nine states do not have casinos). Casinos are built on a massive scale and often incorporate theme parks. There is a wide choice of games including roulette, blackjack, punto banco, poker and dice. Many casinos are open twenty-four hours a day.

Selecting a casino

The amount you have budgeted for will largely determine the sort of club you frequent. The minimum stakes for betting can vary quite considerably in different casinos. Generally, the more upmarket the club, the higher the stakes will be. You will therefore need to consider how many chips of the minimum stake your budget will purchase and how long they will last.

On roulette, in a casino with a £5 minimum bet, a budget of £50 will buy you ten chips. With one spin per minute on American roulette, your money may last only ten minutes. You will also have a limited choice of tables to play on. There may only be one or two tables where you can play the minimum bets, and the low stake tables are always the most crowded in the casino. You may have a long wait before you can get a seat and you will often have to push your way through the other players just to get your bets on.

If, however, you play in a casino with a 25p minimum, £50 will buy you 200 chips. By betting one chip per spin you can play for over three hours. If the 25p table is particularly busy, you will still be able to play for over one-and-a-half hours on a 50p table.

Dress code

Many casinos impose dress codes, particularly the more upmarket establishments. You may be refused admittance if you do not meet the required standard.

Before you go to a casino

Before you go to a casino, learn how to play the games. This may seem like common sense advice but so many people go along and gamble with little or no knowledge about the games they are playing. Losing all your money can prove an expensive lesson.

Work out a budget and stick to it. Only take with you what you can comfortably afford to lose. When you have lost money it's tempting to try to win it back, so leave all your cheque books and credit cards at home. If you can't get your hands on any more money, you won't go over budget.

Tricks casinos use to get you to spend more money

Casinos employ lots of subtle methods to get as much money as possible from you. These include things such as:

- using car jockeys to park your car
- having no clocks or external windows in the gambling area
- using plastic chips instead of money
- supplying free refreshments
- ensuring you walk past amusement machines.

Car jockeys
By employing car jockeys, casinos can ensure you spend more time in the casino. Why make you spend fifteen minutes finding a parking space when you could spend that time gambling?

No clocks or exterior windows

It is common practice not to have any clocks or exterior windows in the gaming rooms. This ensures that you lose track of time.

Using plastic chips

By using plastic chips the casino takes away the association you have with money. If you see a pile of money, you can judge its value. A pile of chips looks worthless.

Free refreshments

Free refreshments are often supplied to keep you in the casino. The longer you spend there the more money you are likely to gamble. In addition, alcohol lowers your inhibitions making you less likely to care if you are losing. It also affects your ability to concentrate which means you take longer to make decisions which can badly affect your playing of the game.

Amusement machines

These will be strategically placed to ensure that you have to walk past them before leaving the casino. Their flashing lights, loud noises and bright colours are designed to attract your attention. You may have lost all your bank notes on the tables but the casino operators know that you may still have a pocket full of change. However, for the serious gambler they are not worth playing as the returns are poor. The house advantage can be as high as fifteen or twenty per cent.

The chips

Instead of playing with money, you purchase plastic chips. There are two types of chips in a casino – cash chips and table chips. Cash chips are a general currency which can be used on any of the games.

You can either exchange your money for chips at the cashpoint or on one of the gaming tables. Dealers are not allowed to take anything from a player's hand, so you simply place the money in front of you on the table and inform the dealer that you want to buy some chips. Don't put the money on the layout, where bets are placed, as some casinos accept bets in cash and may assume that you are placing a bet.

Table chips are found on games like roulette. Each roulette table has its own set of coloured chips. They can only be used on the table you have purchased them from. When you leave the table, any remaining table chips should be given to the dealer who will exchange them for cash chips. It is always best to play with table chips on roulette because if two players are betting with cash chips disputes can arise over whose bet is on the winning number. Each player has different coloured chips.

The value of table chips is automatically the minimum bet on that table. If a player wants them to have a higher value, this will be agreed with the dealer. The dealer will then mark those chips at the higher amount. Typically, round amounts are used – £5, £10, £25, £50, £100 and £400.

When you have finished playing, you take your cash chips to the cash point where they will be exchanged either for cash or a cheque.

Betting with cash

Some casinos allow players to bet by placing money directly on the layout. The dealer will usually exchange the money for a marker.

Minimum and maximum bets

A sign will indicate the table's minimum and maximum bets and the odds payable for each type of bet. The minimum stakes on each table will vary. The lower stake tables are generally busy with lots of people crowded around and at some tables it can be difficult to place your bets. The higher stake tables are generally quieter. Most casinos also have private rooms (salon privé) which are usually for players betting high stakes.

The odds

For a gambler the term 'odds' has two different meanings, depending on the context in which it is used.

1 Chances of winning or losing

Before making a bet you will want to know your chances of winning or losing. In this context the 'odds' is a comparison of the chances of winning and losing and is expressed as a ratio.

Consider the tossing of a coin. There are two possible outcomes – the coin could land on either heads or tails. Suppose two people, we'll call them A and B, decided to bet on the tossing of a coin. A predicts it will land on heads and B thinks it will land on tails. They each bet £10 and agree that the person predicting the correct outcome wins the money.

The coin lands on heads so A wins a total of £20 (£10 from B and the £10 he staked) and B loses £10. A has made a £10 profit and B has made a £10 loss. This is gambling in its simplest form. The amount of money that each player risked was £10. This is called the stake. For A there was one chance that he would lose and one chance that he would win. As a ratio this is 1/1 or odds of one to one. Where the odds are 1/1, it is called even money.

This can be applied to any game to find the chances of winning. Suppose A and B were to bet on the throwing of a six-sided die. Here, there are six possible outcomes. Numbers 1, 2, 3, 4, 5 or 6 could be thrown. If A were to bet on throwing a six, he would have five chances of losing and only one chance of winning (if he threw a 1, 2, 3, 4 or 5 he would lose). The odds against him winning would be 5/1 (five to one).

To calculate the odds in any game, you need to work out how many chances you have of winning and how many of losing.

2 Winnings compared to stakes

The term 'odds' is also applied to the ratio of winnings compared to stakes. In the coin tossing example, A had the chance of winning £10 for a £10 stake. Expressed as a ratio this is 10/10 or 1/1 (even money). Here, the odds against winning are the same as the odds paid. In other words, the true mathematical odds are being paid.

House advantage

If casinos paid out the true odds for every game, they would not make a profit. The casinos, therefore, make a charge for playing the games. They do this in two ways. With some bets they charge a commission, but with most games they adjust the odds paid for winning bets.

With roulette, the odds paid for a bet on en plein (one number) are 35/1. However, the true odds are 36/1. So, for each spin the casino has one number working in its favour. The house advantage is 2.7 per cent of the stakes. So for every £37 that you bet, the casino is raking off £1.

The house advantage varies with different games and casinos. It is therefore worth shopping around for the best deal. With games like dice/craps, the type of bet can make a huge impact on the house advantage. Some bets cut the house advantage to under 1 per cent whereas others give the house a massive 16.67 per cent.

Before you place a bet find out the house advantage, not just for the game as a whole but also for the individual bets. Some bets are simply not worth playing because you are at such a huge disadvantage.

2
ROULETTE

Roulette is a game of chance played on a spinning numbered wheel and is one of the most popular casino games played. The numbers zero to 36 are arranged around a wheel on numbered slots. Each number is coloured either red or black, except for zero which is green. The dealer spins the ball around the wheel in the opposite direction to which the wheel is turning, and players bet on which number the ball will land in. Diamond shaped bars are set at intervals around the wheel. If the ball hits one of the bars it will be deflected off at a different angle, thus making it more difficult to predict the winning number.

The wheel

There are two different types of wheel: the European wheel and the American wheel. In Great Britain and Europe a European style wheel is used. All the numbers are randomly arranged with one zero. In addition, the wheels used for American and French roulette differ slightly. French roulette wheels incorporate spikes so that the direction of the wheel can be changed. With American roulette, the wheel continually spins in the same direction.

In the United States a wheel with two zeros (0 and 00) is used. The numbers are arranged with consecutive numbers opposite one another.

Occassionally you may see a table with a double layout, this does not affect the playing of the game.

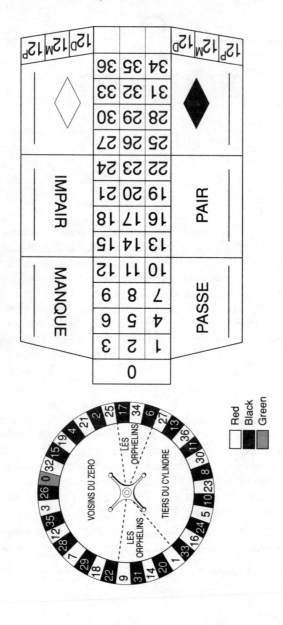

Figure 2.1 The European wheel and betting layout for French roulette

00	3	6	9	12	15	18	21	24	27	30	33	36	2 to 1
	2	5	8	11	14	17	20	23	26	29	32	35	2 to 1
0	1	4	7	10	13	16	19	22	25	28	31	34	2 to 1

	1st 12		2nd 12		3rd 12	
	1 to 18	EVEN	RED	BLACK	ODD	19 to 36

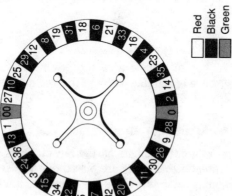

Red
Black
Green

Figure 2.2 The American wheel and betting layout for American roulette

The type of wheel you play on can affect your chances of winning. The two zeros on American wheels give the house a 5.26 per cent advantage, whereas the continental wheels with only one zero give the house a 2.7 per cent advantage. If possible you should try to play on tables where only one zero is used.

American and French roulette

The games, though basically the same, differ in some aspects. American roulette is a much faster game than French roulette. The dealers use their hands to move the chips around whereas a rake is used in French roulette. The layouts also differ (see Figures 2.1 and 2.2).

If you have the choice, it is better to play French roulette as you have more time in between spins to decide where to bet.

The bets

There are many different kinds of bets which can be played (see Figure 2.3).

(a) En plein

A bet on a single number. The chip should be placed directly on top of the number, ensuring that it does not touch any lines. Odds paid are 35/1.

(b) Cheval or split

A bet on two adjacent numbers on the layout. The bet should be placed on the centre of the line between the two numbers. Odds paid are 17/1.

(c) Transversale plein or street

A bet on three adjacent numbers on the layout. Odds paid are 11/1. On American roulette these bets are placed on the side of the layout that has the double line. As well as the numbers running across the layout (see (c)(i) on page 13), it is also possible to play the numbers 0/1/2 (see (c)(ii) on page 13) and 0/2/3.

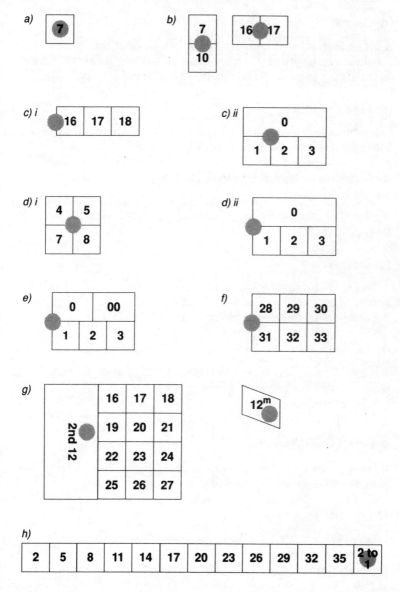

Figure 2.3 The different kinds of bets and where to place them

(d) Carre

A bet on four adjacent numbers on the layout. Odds paid are 8/1. The bet should be played on the intersection of the four numbers. A carre on 0/1/2/3 is commonly called the first four (see (d)(ii) on page 13).

(e) Five numbers

When roulette is played with two zeros, it is possible to make a bet on 0/00/1/2/3. Odds paid are 6/1.

(f) Sixainne or transversale simple

A bet on six adjacent numbers on the layout. With American roulette the bet should be placed on the side of the layout with double lines. Odds paid are 5/1.

(g) Dozen

A bet on twelve numbers. The first dozen is the numbers 1–12, the second dozen is the numbers 13–24 inclusive and the third dozen is the numbers 25–36 inclusive. Odds paid are 2/1.

(h) Column

A bet on the columns of twelve numbers running along the table. The second column is a bet on the numbers 2/5/8/11/14/17/20/23/26/29/32/35. Odds paid are 2/1.

Even chance bets

All of these bets pay odds of evens (1/1) (see Figure 2.4). The chips are placed in the appropriate marked box.

(i) Low/manque

A bet on the low numbers 1–18 inclusive.

(j) Even/pair

A bet on the even numbers.

(k) Red

A bet on all the red numbers.

(l) Black

A bet on all the black numbers.

(m) Odd/impair

A bet on all the odd numbers.

(n) High/passe

A bet on the high numbers 19–36 inclusive.

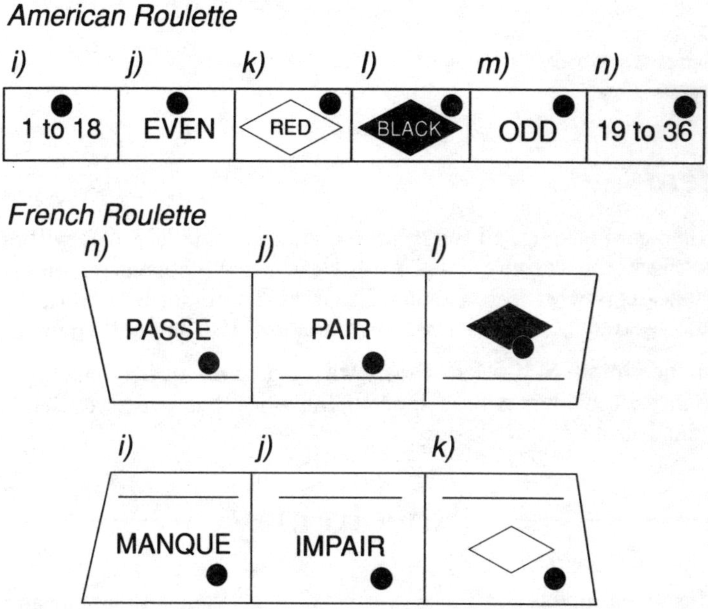

Figure 2.4 Where to place even chance bets

Badly placed bets

Ensure that your bets are placed exactly on the correct bet. If a chip intended for an en plein is touching the line, it will be paid out as a cheval (see Figure 2.5). Bets which are not exactly placed may be straightened up by the dealer who will call out the colour of the chip and the number(s) that it is covering. It is therefore important to pay attention to the dealer, otherwise your bets may not be placed where you intended.

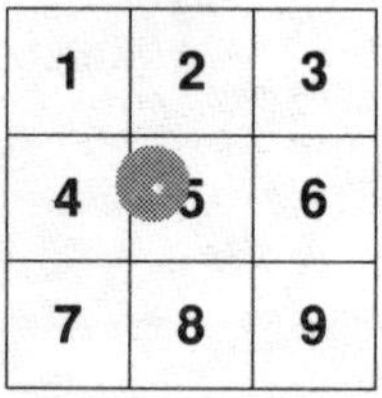

1	2	3
4	5	6
7	8	9

If there is another player's bet on the number(s) that you want, simply place your chips on top of his.

Figure 2.5 A badly placed bet

Zero

When zero is spun, all the column and dozen bets lose. You will need to check the casino's rules to discover what happens to the even chance bets when zero is spun. In Great Britain all bets on the even chances (red, black, odd, even, high and low) lose half of their stake.

In the United States, on wheels with one zero, all bets on the even chances lose when zero is spun. If the wheel has two zeros, half the stake is lost.

How to play

The dealer announces 'Place your bets' which signals that you can put your chips in the appropriate places on the layout. The ball is spun. As it slows down, 'No more bets' is announced. Any bets placed after this announcement may be returned by the dealer.

The dealer calls out the winning number, also stating the colour and whether or not it is even or odd. For example, number 17 would be announced as '17 black odd'.

A marker called a dolly is placed on the winning number and losing bets are cleared away. Winning bets are paid out in a pre-determined order. When all winning bets have been paid the dealer will remove the dolly and call out 'Place your bets', signalling that new bets can be placed.

Order of payout

Winning bets are paid out in a pre-set order as follows: Column, even chances and dozen are paid first. The bets around the winning number are then spread out to make them easier to see. The bets furthest from the wheel are paid first, ending with the en pleins.

If you have several chips on different bets around the number, the winnings will be totalled and paid together. Your winning bets may be as follows:

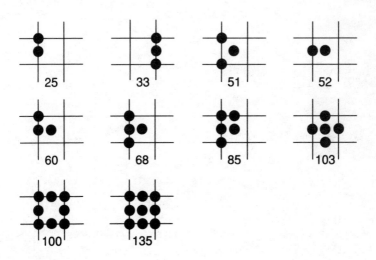

Figure 2.6 Using pictures to calculate winnings

Three sixainnes at 5/1
One carre at 8/1
Two chevals at 17/1
Four en pleins at 35/1.

The dealer will announce the colour of your chips and the total number of chips – in this example 197.

The dealer will then make up your payout. Unless you specifically request your payout to be made up in a certain way, the dealer will estimate how many chips you need to play with and make up your payout accordingly.

You should always check the payout to ensure it is correct. If you have any queries about your payouts or the dealing of the game you should speak to the inspector who will be watching the table. Most disputes are easily settled by referring to the video cameras that record all the action in the casino.

3

TIPS FOR PLAYING ROULETTE

First of all, familiarise yourself with the layout as once people start playing the numbers quickly get covered with chips and it can be difficult to work out where all the numbers are. Never move another player's chips. If you are unsure where to place a particular bet, you can always ask the dealer where the number is or, alternatively, ask him to place the bet for you.

Try to sit opposite the dealer in the middle of the table. Here you will easily be able to reach the entire layout. If you can't reach the numbers you want to bet on, your chips should be placed on the table in front of you and the bet called out to the dealer. The dealer will repeat your bet to confirm the details. Never throw chips at the layout as this only serves to knock other bets from the correct position. As mentioned in the previous chapter, be sure to place your bets in exactly the correct place.

The law of averages

Many gamblers rely on the law of averages – that in the long run all numbers will be spun an equal amount of times. However, the law of averages is a fallacy. Consider the tossing of a coin. If a coin lands on heads on the first toss does this mean the second toss will be tails? The answer is 'possibly' since there is a 50 per cent chance that it could land on either side.

Suppose you tossed the coin 100 times. What result would you expect? According to the law of averages, it would be 50 times heads and 50 times tails because in the long run it would even out. But just because there is a 50 per cent chance of something happening, it doesn't mean it will happen 50 per cent of the time. The coin does not know what the previous result was. Each subsequent toss is totally unrelated to the previous toss. There is no reason why you couldn't throw 100 heads or 100 tails in a row.

With roulette some players bet on numbers that have failed to appear because the law of averages says that they should eventually be spun. However, it has been known for some numbers not to appear at certain tables for weeks. By waiting for one particular number that has not appeared for a while, you can easily lose a lot of money.

Detecting a bias in the wheel

Go into any casino and you will see players marking the number after each spin. Some sit for hours marking the numbers for a particular wheel in the hope that a pattern will emerge. Some players even claim to have the entire records for a particular wheel for several years. What they are trying to do is to detect a bias in the wheel.

This system was successfully used by William Jaggers at the end of the nineteenth century. In those days the roulette wheels were crudely made and not balanced. He found that the ball was landing more often in one section of the wheel and won by playing those numbers.

Today, roulette wheels are precision made and their balance is checked every day. Any bias is going to be minute and hardly worth bothering with. Casino operators know that it is virtually impossible to detect any bias. They even provide pencils and cards so that the players can note the numbers. On some tables the previous numbers spun are electronically displayed.

To detect such a bias involves hours of collecting and analysing the numbers spun. As soon as a wheel is re-balanced or serviced, the data previously collected becomes useless. However, this does not dissuade players from looking.

Detecting a bias in the dealer

Rather than detect a bias in the wheel, another alternative is to look for a bias in the dealer's spin. The wheel is virtually the same, dealers aren't.

Casinos know that if a dealer continually spins the ball at the same speed, it will tend to land in the same area of the wheel. This is why dealers are taught to vary their spin. However, dealers are only human. There are good and bad dealers. Those who are conscientious will ensure that every spin differs. Other dealers can't be bothered and don't always vary their spin. When they're dealing a game of roulette, they get into a natural rhythm. The central wheel tends to get spun at the same speed; they get into the knack of pulling it at an optimum rate; and they have plenty of other things to think about apart from varying their spin.

If this happens, it is quite common for the same number to appear twice. This is why a lot of players let their winning bets ride for the next spin. Spinning the same number twice usually alerts the dealer that he should vary his spin. Also, if an inspector notices that the ball keeps on hitting the same section of the wheel, the dealer will be reminded to vary his spin.

The size of the ball can also make a difference to where it lands. Small balls tend to bounce a lot. If a small ball is being used, ask the inspector to change it for a bigger one. They are usually happy to oblige.

Look for a dealer who tends to spin the ball in the same area of the wheel in consecutive spins and start gathering data. If a dealer is tending to spin neighbours then the odds can be in your favour. Ideally look for a slower dealer as you have more time to think about your bets in between spins.

If you can find a dealer who is spinning balls into the same area on the wheel, there are several bets that can be played that will cover sections of the wheels.

– Bets covering sections of the wheel –

It is common for players to bet on particular sections of the wheel. Most bets of this type have been developed on the European wheel.

Neighbour bets

Neighbour bets are very popular. A section of five numbers on the wheel is played. The bet is called out as 'neighbours' of the central number. One chip is placed on each number as an en plein bet. Seventeen and the neighbours would be an en plein bet on each of the numbers 2, 25, 17, 34 and 6.

In most casinos the dealer will place the bet for you. You simply give the dealer five chips and announce 'seventeen and the neighbours'. The dealer will repeat the bet and place one chip on each of the numbers 2, 25, 17, 34 and 6.

Figure 3.1 The neighbours of 17

To speed up the placing of neighbour bets, some layouts include an oval-shaped representation of the wheel. These bets are placed by the dealer. All of the chips will be put on the box marked 17. The dealer will call out the winning number and place the dolly as usual. He will then point out the number on the oval and either call out 'neighbours win' or 'neighbours lose'. If you have the winning number, one of the chips will be taken from the oval and placed on the winning number. The bet will then be dealt with in the usual payout order.

Some casinos do not allow call bets, and in these instances it will usually be stated on the sign above the table. You can still play neighbour bets but it means you have to place the chips yourself on the relevant numbers.

If this is your preferred method of play, you will find it useful to memorise the order of the numbers on the wheel. Alternatively, you may prefer to use the charts given on pages 23 and 24.

Neighbours on a continental wheel

12	35	3	26	**0**	32	15	19	4
5	24	16	33	**1**	20	14	31	9
15	19	4	21	**2**	25	17	34	6
7	28	12	35	**3**	26	0	32	15
0	32	15	19	**4**	21	2	25	17
30	8	23	10	**5**	24	16	33	1
2	25	17	34	**6**	27	13	36	11
9	22	18	29	**7**	28	12	35	3
13	36	11	30	**8**	23	10	5	24
1	20	14	31	**9**	22	18	29	7
11	30	8	23	**10**	5	24	16	33
6	27	13	36	**11**	30	8	23	10
18	29	7	28	**12**	35	3	26	0
17	34	6	27	**13**	36	11	30	8
16	33	1	20	**14**	31	9	22	18
3	26	0	32	**15**	19	4	21	2
23	10	5	24	**16**	33	1	20	14
4	21	2	25	**17**	34	6	27	13
14	31	9	22	**18**	29	7	28	12
26	0	32	15	**19**	4	21	2	25
24	16	33	1	**20**	14	31	9	22
32	15	19	4	**21**	2	25	17	34
20	14	31	9	**22**	18	29	7	28
36	11	30	8	**23**	10	5	24	16
8	23	10	5	**24**	16	33	1	20
19	4	21	2	**25**	17	34	6	27
28	12	35	3	**26**	0	32	15	19
25	17	34	6	**27**	13	36	11	30
22	18	29	7	**28**	12	35	3	26
31	9	22	18	**29**	7	28	12	35
27	13	36	11	**30**	8	23	10	5
33	1	20	14	**31**	9	22	18	29
35	3	26	0	**32**	15	19	4	21
10	5	24	16	**33**	1	20	14	31
21	2	25	17	**34**	6	27	13	36
29	7	28	12	**35**	3	26	0	32
34	6	27	13	**36**	11	30	8	23

Neighbours on a US wheel

24	36	13	1	**00**	27	10	25	29
3	24	36	13	**1**	00	27	10	25
4	23	35	14	**2**	0	28	9	26
5	22	34	15	**3**	24	36	13	1
6	21	33	16	**4**	23	35	14	2
7	20	32	17	**5**	22	34	15	3
8	19	31	18	**6**	21	33	16	4
9	26	30	11	**7**	20	32	17	5
10	25	29	12	**8**	19	31	18	6
14	2	0	28	**9**	26	30	11	7
13	1	00	27	**10**	25	29	12	8
28	9	26	30	**11**	7	20	32	17
27	10	25	29	**12**	8	19	31	18
15	3	24	36	**13**	1	00	27	10
16	4	23	35	**14**	2	0	28	9
17	5	22	34	**15**	3	24	36	13
18	6	21	33	**16**	4	23	35	14
11	7	20	32	**17**	5	22	34	15
12	8	19	31	**18**	6	21	33	16
25	29	12	8	**19**	31	18	6	21
26	30	11	7	**20**	32	17	5	22
19	31	18	6	**21**	33	16	4	23
20	32	17	5	**22**	34	15	3	24
21	33	16	4	**23**	35	14	2	0
22	34	15	3	**24**	36	13	1	00
1	00	27	10	**25**	29	12	8	19
2	0	28	9	**26**	30	11	7	20
36	13	1	00	**27**	10	25	29	12
35	14	2	0	**28**	9	26	30	11
00	27	10	25	**29**	12	8	19	31
0	28	9	26	**30**	11	7	20	32
29	12	8	19	**31**	18	6	21	33
30	11	7	20	**32**	17	5	22	34
31	18	6	21	**33**	16	4	23	35
32	17	5	22	**34**	15	3	24	36
33	16	4	23	**35**	14	2	0	28
34	15	3	24	**36**	13	1	00	27

Several other bets that are played on European wheels are common in British and continental casinos. You can either place the bets yourself or if call bets are accepted, give the dealer the necessary number of chips.

Tiers du cylindre

Tiers du cylindre is commonly called 'tiers'. It is a six piece bet of six chevals (see page 12), covering the numbers 5/8, 10/11, 13/16, 23/24, 27/30, 33/36.

This bet ensures almost one third of the wheel is played from the number 33 to 27. If any number in that section is spun, seventeen chips are won and five chips are lost.

Voisins du zero

Voisins du zero is a nine piece bet covering the section of the wheel around zero. The bets placed are 0/2/3 (2 pieces) transversale plein (see page 12); 4/7 cheval; 12/15 cheval; 18/21 cheval; 19/22 cheval; 25/29 (2 pieces) carre (see page 14) and 32/35 cheval.

If the numbers 0, 2, 3, 25, 26, 28 or 29 win, sixteen chips are won and eight chips are lost. If any of the other numbers win, seventeen chips are won and eight chips are lost.

Les orphelins

Les orphelins (the orphans) is a bet on the two sections of the wheel not covered by the tiers and the voisins du zero. It is a five piece bet on number 1 (en plein), and the chevals 6/9, 14/17, 17/20, 31/34. If number 1 wins, 35 chips are won and four are lost. If number 17 wins, 34 chips are won and three chips are lost. If 6, 9, 14, 20, 31 or 34 win, seventeen chips are won and four chips are lost.

—————— Staking systems ——————

In British casinos, betting on the even money chances provides the best value for money. Since only half the stake is lost if zero is spun, they give a house advantage of only 1.35 per cent. Whilst you might

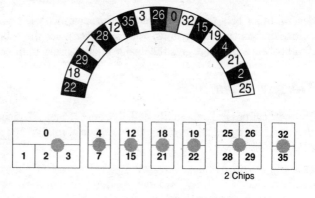

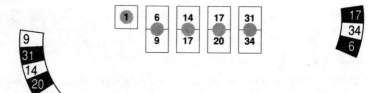

Les orphelins

Tiers du cylindre

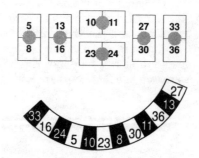

Figure 3.2 Different kinds of neighbour bets

be able to deduce which part of the wheel the winning number will be in, it is almost impossible to predict whether the number will be odd, even, high, low, red or black. Another disadvantage of playing these bets is that low odds are paid which means it takes a long time to accumulate winnings.

To get around this difficulty of predicting whether a number will be red or black etc., many systems have been invented to take the decision away from the player. Some of the more popular ones are described here.

The martingale system

This system is used for betting on the even money chances (even, odd, high, low, red and black). Stakes are doubled after a loss.

Suppose you wanted to bet on red. You would wait until several black numbers have appeared consecutively. You would then place a bet on red. If it loses, the stake is doubled. If that bet loses the stake is again doubled. The system relies on you always being able to recoup your losses because a red number will eventually be spun.

If you win, you wait until there is another sequence of black numbers and start betting again.

The main problem is the amount of capital that is needed. There may be a run of nine successive black numbers. If your original stake is £1, you would need capital in excess of £1000. However, if red fails to appear on the tenth spin, your next bet would need to be over £2000 which may be approaching the table maximum, depending on the casino. Once the maximum bet has been reached, you can no longer double up.

The labouchere system

The labouchere system is used for betting on the even money chances. It involves crossing out numbers from the top and bottom of a sequence of numbers to determine what the stake will be.

The numbers 1 to 4 are written down. The first and last numbers in the sequence are added to find the stake.

If you win you cross out the first and last numbers and stake the amount given by adding the new first and last numbers. If you lose you put your last stake at the end of the sequence of numbers and add the first and last numbers to determine your new stake.

When all of the numbers have been crossed out, you write down the numbers 1 to 4 and start again. The problem with this system is that a losing sequence can soon wipe out both your winnings and your capital.

Example of the labouchere system

	Stake	Win/lose	Capital
1234	5	win	+5
23	5	lose	–
235	7	win	+7
3	3	lose	+4
33	6	win	+10
1234	5	lose	+5
12345	6	lose	–1
123456	7	lose	–8
1234567	8	lose	–16

The reverse labouchere system

The systems looked at so far involve risking a lot of capital for small gains. The reverse labouchere differs because it risks a small amount of capital for potentially huge gains.

It involves betting on the even money chances. The same principle is used as the labouchere for determining the stakes, but instead of increasing bets after a loss, they are increased after a win. Once you hit a winning streak, you are effectively playing with the bank's money rather than your own stake.

If you do lose, your loses are minimal. However, if you win the returns can be huge. The table maximums represent the limit of the system. Once the table maximum has been reached, you go back to the minimum bet.

Write down the numbers 1 to 4 as follows: 1 2 3 4. Now add the first and last in the sequence to determine the stake. In this case, five units. If the bet wins write the stake at the end of the sequence and again add the first and last to determine the stake. If you lose, cross out the first and last numbers and add the remaining first and last numbers to find the new stake.

When you have crossed out all of the numbers, you start again with the numbers 1 to 4. Each time you cross out all of the numbers you lose 10 chips.

The table below shows what would happen if the reverse labouchere system was used to bet on both red and black. In this sequence red appears fifteen times and black six times. Net winnings = £153.

If there is an equal number of blacks and reds, the system breaks even, unless zero is spun.

Example of the reverse labouchere system – betting on red

Staking sequence	Stake	Win/lose	Cumulative capital
1234	5	w	5
12345	6	w	11
123456	7	w	18
1234567	8	l	10
23456	8	l	2
345	8	l	−6
4	4	w	−2
44	8	w	6
448	12	w	18
448 12	16	w	34
448 12 16	20	w	54
4 4 8 12 16 20	24	w	78
4 4 8 12 16 20 24	28	w	106
4 4 8 12 16 20 24 28	32	l	74
4 8 12 16 20 24	28	l	46
8 12 16 20	28	w	74
8 12 16 20 28	36	w	110
8 12 16 20 28 36	44	w	154
8 12 16 20 28 36 44	52	l	102
12 16 20 28 36	48	w	150
12 16 20 28 36 48	59	w	210

Example of the reverse labouchere system – betting on black

Staking sequence	Stake	Win/lose	Cumulative capital
1234	5	l	–5
23	5	l	–10
1234	5	l	–15
23	5	w	–10
235	7	w	–3
2357	9	w	6
23579	11	l	–5
357	10	l	–15
5	5	l	–20
1234	5	l	–25
23	5	l	–30
1234	5	l	–35
23	5	l	–40
1234	5	w	–35
12345	6	w	–29
123456	7	l	–36
2345	7	l	–43
34	7	l	–50
1234	5	w	–45
12345	6	l	–51
234	6	l	–57

The effect of zero

On the above example, if zero were to come up on spin 21, net winnings would be reduced to £66. If it were to come up on both spins 20 and 21, net winnings would be reduced to £5.

This system, played at its most effective, is carried out on all the even chance bets. However, it is impossible for one person to make all the necessary calculations in the limited space of time between spins.

Owing to the amount of time it takes to accumulate winnings, it is advisable to play as a team. Another alternative is to still place bets on all possibilities but to not bet on every spin. Just bet when you are ready. All that the system relies on is you having a sequence of winning bets. It does not matter on which bet they appear.

4
BLACKJACK

Blackjack is a card game played with several decks of cards, common-ly four or six packs. It is based on the game of 21. Rules may vary in different casinos, so always check them before you start playing. You play only against the dealer, so the other players' hands do not affect your game. To win you need to beat the dealer's hand up to a score not exceeding 21.

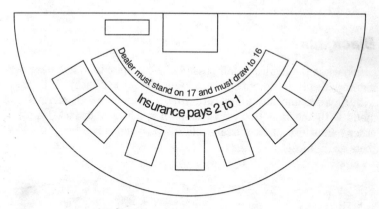

Figure 4.1 The betting layout for blackjack

Card values

All the cards from 2 to 10 inclusive have their face value. The court cards (kings, queens and jacks) have a value of 10. The value of an ace depends on the total score. When an ace is initially dealt, its value is 11. If the player's hand exceeds a score of 21, the ace then has a value of 1.

Scoring

The value of each card in a hand is added to give the player's score.

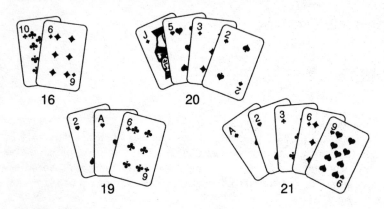

Figure 4.2 Blackjack scores

Blackjack

Blackjack is the highest hand possible, and despite its name has nothing specifically to do with the jacks in the pack. Blackjack is made with any ace and any other card with a value of 10. It can only be made with the first two cards dealt in a hand. Blackjack beats all other hands, except for a dealer blackjack, when it is a tie or standoff (bets are not lost).

Figure 4.3 Ways of making blackjack

Although the total score of blackjack is 21, it beats a score of 21 made up with other combinations of cards, for example, three sevens.

If you have blackjack your bet is immediately paid at odds of 3/2 (one-and-a-half to one) unless the dealer's first card is an ace or worth 10. In this case you would have to wait for the outcome of the dealer's hand.

Because only your first two cards can make blackjack, if you receive an ace and a card worth 10 after splitting (see note on page 34), you will not have blackjack.

How to play

The cards are shuffled by the dealer and cut by the player. They are then placed in a shoe (a box where cards are placed for dealing). A blank card is inserted roughly one deck from the end to indicate when the dealer should re-shuffle the cards.

After placing their initial bets, each player is dealt two cards face up. Players are not allowed to touch the cards. This ensures that the cards do not become marked. The cards are dealt clockwise starting with the player immediately to the left of the dealer. The dealer also receives two cards. In Great Britain, the dealer initially receives one card only. In the United States, the dealer receives two cards, but one is dealt face down.

Players judge their chances of beating the dealer with the cards they hold and the card shown in the dealer's hand. The cards you have compared to the card in the dealer's hand will determine what you do next. You have several options. You can stand (take no further cards); take more cards to try to improve your score; split your cards into two hands by making an additional bet; or you can double your additional bet.

In Great Britain, you will be asked by the dealer if you want another card. To this, you simply reply 'yes' or 'no'. In the United States the procedure is different. To get another card you make a scratching motion on the table. To decline a card, you make a waving motion with your hand.

You can take as many cards as you like to improve your score, but if your score exceeds 21, you lose, and your cards will be cleared away. You still lose even if the dealer's hand exceeds 21. A tie or standoff occurs only if both scores are equal and do not exceed 21.

Once you are satisfied that you have sufficient cards to beat the dealer's eventual score, you should 'stand' (take no more cards).

After all of the players hands have been dealt with, the dealer will turn his attention to his own hand. If his score is 16 or less, he must take a card. If his score goes above 21 he has lost and all the winning bets are paid. Once he reaches 17 or over he must stand (he can't take any more cards). Any players who have beaten the dealer's score are paid. If you tie with the dealer, your bet is a standoff (not lost).

Options

Depending on the initial value of the cards dealt, you have several options available to you.

Doubling

Rules vary as to when you can double, so always check first. In Great Britain, you can make a further bet equal to your initial stake if your first two cards give a score of 9, 10 or 11. Whether or not doubling your bet is a wise move depends on the dealer's score (see the chart 'The best moves to make in blackjack' on pages 37–38). In the United States you may double your initial bet on any score other than black-jack and take only one more card. Check the chart on pages 37–38 for the best scores to double on.

Splitting

After two cards have been dealt, you have the option of splitting them into two separate hands. An additional bet equal to your initial bet can be made. See the chart (pages 37–38) for the best option. In Great Britain cards with a value of 4, 5 or 10 each are excluded. You would not want to split these cards anyway. If two aces are split into two hands only one extra card can be taken. If you split two aces and then get a 10 value card – this is not blackjack as you can only have black-jack after two cards have been dealt. Instead you have a score of 21.

Odds paid

If both the dealer and the player have the same score, the bet is a standoff (not lost).

If a player wins with a score of 21 with two cards only (blackjack) the odds are 3/2.

If the player beats the dealer on any other score the odds are 1/1 (even).

Insurance pays 2/1.

Insurance

Insurance is an additional bet you can make if you have blackjack and the dealer's first card is an ace. Here, you make a further bet equal to half your original stake. If the dealer has blackjack, your original bet loses but your insurance bet is paid at odds of 2/1. If the dealer does not have blackjack, you lose the insurance bet, but your original bet is paid at 3/2.

When you take insurance, the outcome is the same whether the dealer has blackjack or not. Your net winnings are even money. Some casinos automatically pay you even money as soon as you take insurance.

Two or more players betting on one box

It is possible to bet on other players' hands by placing a bet in their box. However, you have no control over the hands. The original player makes all the decisions. However, if the controlling player decides to split, double, or take insurance, you do not have to. If hands are split, you have to nominate which hand your bet is on.

Betting on another player's box can be useful if you are learning the game and are not yet confident in your own ability as a player. However, as the other player will be making all the decisions, it is wise to bet with a shrewd player.

Where to place bets

You can bet on as many boxes as you like, up to the table maximum. You can either play yourself or bet on other players' hands. Chips must be placed in the correct position.

● for single bets, chips should be placed in the box;
● for split bets, chips should be placed on the line of the box;
● for doubled bets, chips should be placed behind the original stake;

- for double split bets, chips should be placed behind original stakes on the line;
- for two bets, chips should be placed side by side in the box;
- for two bets split, chips should be placed behind each other on the line of the box;
- for two bets doubled and split, chips should be placed on top of the existing split bets.

It is important to keep track of where you place your bets as, unlike roulette, players use cash chips. It is therefore possible for disputes to arise over which bets belong to which person. If disputes do arise they are easily resolved by referring to the camera.

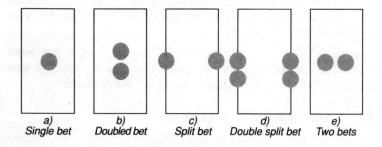

| a) | b) | c) | d) | e) |
| Single bet | Doubled bet | Split bet | Double split bet | Two bets |

Figure 4.4 Where to place bets

5

TIPS FOR PLAYING BLACKJACK

Practise as much as possible. You can easily recreate the game at home. The chart below shows the best moves to make. Try playing the game at home with the chart beside you, checking each move. With practice you will remember the best options.

The best moves to make in blackjack

C Take a card; – stand; D Double; S Split

Player's hand	Dealer's card									
	2	3	4	5	6	7	8	9	10	Ace
8	C	C	C	C	C	C	C	C	C	C
9	C	D	D	D	D	C	C	C	C	C
10	D	D	D	D	D	D	D	D	C	C
11	D	D	D	D	D	D	D	D	D	C
12	C	C	–	–	–	C	C	C	C	C
13	–	–	–	–	–	C	C	C	C	C
14	–	–	–	–	–	C	C	C	C	C
15	–	–	–	–	–	C	C	C	C	C
16	–	–	–	–	–	C	C	C	C	C
Ace 2	C	C	C	C	D	D	C	C	C	C
Ace 3	C	C	C	D	D	C	C	C	C	C
Ace 4	C	C	D	D	D	C	C	C	C	C
Ace 5	C	C	D	D	D	C	C	C	C	C
Ace 6	C	D	D	D	D	C	C	C	C	C
Ace 7	–	–	–	–	–	–	–	C	C	C

Player's hand	Dealer's card									
Ace 8	–	–	–	–	–	–				
–	–	–	–							
Ace 9	–	–	–	–	–	–	–	–	–	–
Ace Ace	S	S	S	S	S	S	S	S	S	S
2 2	S	S	S	S	S	S	C	C	C	C
3 3	S	S	S	S	S	S	C	C	C	C
4 4	C	C	C	C	C	C	C	C	C	C
6 6	S	S	S	S	S	C	C	C	C	C
7 7	S	S	S	S	S	S	C	C	C	C
8 8	S	S	S	S	S	S	S	S	S	–
9 9	S	S	S	S	S	–	S	S	–	–
10 10	–	–	–	–	–	–	–	–	–	–

Scoring 16

Lots of players make the mistake of standing on 16 when the dealer has a 7 or higher. The best option is always to take another card. You stand more chance of winning by taking an extra card than you do by standing.

——— Card counting ———

Take a pack of cards, shuffle them and split them into two equal piles. Count how many cards with a value of 10 (referred to as 'tens') are in each half. If you do this several times, you will see that the number of tens in each half can vary considerably. This is the basis of most card counting techniques. As a player of blackjack it is to your advantage to know when the remaining cards are rich in tens.

On average, the house advantage on blackjack is 5.6 per cent. However, a situation can arise when the house no longer has an advantage. This depends on what cards are left in the shoe. If there are lots of tens left in the shoe, the odds are in the player's favour. By counting the cards, you can calculate when this situation arises. The most widely used system is to determine when the shoe is rich in tens. This is because dealers must draw extra cards if their score is below 17, but players can stand on any score. If the deck is rich is tens, the dealer stands more chance of busting. Once this situation arises, you can take advantage by increasing your stakes.

Suppose a dealer's first card is a 6 and the second card has a value of 10. The dealer has a score of 16, so must take another card. If there are lots of tens in the shoe, the next card is more likely to be a 10 – giving the dealer a score of 26. A player, however, can stand on a score of 16.

Even the dealer's chances of scoring 20 do not place the player at a disadvantage. They each have an equal chance of scoring 20. A player can also increase his chances of scoring 20 by playing more boxes. If a player bets on all seven boxes, he will have seven chances of scoring 20 compared with only one for the dealer.

Although fewer decks of cards make the counting easier, because the numbers involved are smaller, it can actually be in the player's favour if a greater number of decks are used. If four packs of cards are used and the player realises at the halfway point that they are rich in tens, fewer hands can be played than if six decks are used.

If you decide to use a card counting system, try to find a slow dealer as you have more time to make your calculations. It is also advantageous to sit on the anchor box (the last hand to be dealt). This is because you will see more cards before your hand is dealt. You are in control of the game because you decide what card the dealer gets (you are the last player who has the opportunity to take cards, therefore the dealer's card is dependent on how many cards you take).

Keeping track of the tens

The simplest method is to count the tens when they appear. You can judge when you are roughly half-way through the shoe. In four decks there are 64 cards with a value of 10, and in six decks there are 96 cards. So, if you are playing with four decks and by the half-way point fewer than 32 cards with a value of 10 have appeared, you know that the remaining cards are rich in tens. You can then increase your bets and/or play more boxes. If the cards are poor in tens, you can decrease your stakes or stop playing.

The starting point for counting tens	
Number of decks	*Number of cards with a value of ten*
1	16
2	32
3	48
4	64
5	80
6	96

Keeping track of the tens and low cards

This system is more accurate because it also takes into account the low value cards which could ruin the previous system if the dealer continually draws them. It involves keeping a running total in your head which requires a high level of concentration.

Every time an ace or a card worth 10 is dealt count –1 (minus one). When numbers 2 to 6 are dealt count +1 (plus one). A plus figure means the deck is rich in tens. When this situation arises bets can be increased and/or more boxes played. If there is a minus or low figure either reduce the stakes or stop playing.

Calculating the ratio of tens to other cards

This is more accurate than the previous system but it requires a great deal of mental dexterity and a lot of practice to perfect. Calculations have to be made quickly and accurately.

In a deck of cards there are 16 cards with a value of 10 and 36 other cards. The ratio of other cards to tens is 36/16 = 2.25. When the ratio falls below this level the deck is rich in tens.

Using the system

Count the number of unseen tens and count the number of unseen others. With four decks, the starting point for the tens is 64 and the others 144. Deduct one from each total as a relevant card is seen. Divide the unseen others by the unseen tens. If the number is less than 2.25, the deck is rich in tens. Stakes can be increased and/or more boxes played when this situation is reached. A number higher than 2.25 means that the deck is poor in tens. In this instance you should decrease the stakes or stop playing.

Example 1
Unseen tens = 50
Unseen others - 100
Ratio = 100/50 = 2

Here the deck is rich in tens. Bets should be increased.

Example 2
Unseen tens = 40
Unseen others = 120
Ratio = 120/40 = 3

Here the deck is poor in tens. Bets should be reduced.

Counting fives

An alternative system is to count fives. When the remaining cards are poor in fives the player has the advantage.

Count the number of unseen fives and the number of unseen others. Divide the number of unseen others by the number of unseen fives.

If the ratio is above 13, increase stakes and/or play more boxes. If the ratio is below 13 decrease stakes or stop playing.

Starting points for calculating unseen fives and unseen others		
Number of decks	*Unseen fives*	*Unseen others*
1	4	48
2	8	96
3	12	144
4	16	192
5	20	240
6	24	288

Example 1
Unseen others = 100
Unseen fives = 10
Ratio = 100/10 => 10

Here the deck is rich in fives, so bets should be reduced.

Example 2
Unseen others = 90
Unseen fives = 6
Ratio = 90/6 => 15

Here the deck is poor in fives, so bets should be increased.

Casinos' reactions to card counters

For obvious reasons, casinos don't like card counters and will do everything in their power to deter them. If they suspect you of card counting, they will make it very difficult for you to continue. They may employ the tactic of distracting your attention, or destroying your chances by insisting that the cards are shuffled more often. Casinos reserve the right to shuffle the cards at any time. If you win lots of money, they may simply ask you to leave. Another problem is that casinos share information about card counters, so if you get barred from one casino, you could find yourself barred from many other local casinos.

To avoid this situation, you need to attract as little attention as possible. On your initial visit to a casino, you will be assessed. If your stakes are small, you will be virtually ignored. If you also play when the casino is at its busiest, you will go unnoticed.

If you play small stakes but then hugely increase your stakes towards the end of shoe and continually win, you will arouse suspicion. It can therefore help if you develop an erratic betting pattern. Some players, however, try for a big hit. They play big stakes in an attempt to win as much as possible before being thrown out.

Another method to employ is to work as a team with another player. One person watches a game in progress and counts the cards. A signal alerts a second person that a shoe is rich in tens. The second person comes to the table and starts playing. This way you have avoided betting when the shoe is not in your favour.

You can usually spot when you are under suspicion if the pit boss starts watching your game. However, it is not always obvious as your game can be watched from the camera room. If you think you may have attracted attention, it is best to change to another casino before enough evidence is gathered to throw you out.

Variations on the basic game of blackjack

Some casinos offer additional bets that can be played on blackjack.

Surrender blackjack

This gives you the opportunity to cut your losses when you have a poor hand. After your first two cards have been dealt you have the option to discontinue playing your hand and surrender half of your stake. However, if the dealer has blackjack then you lose all of your stake.

Over/under 13

This is an additional bet. You can bet that your first two cards will be either over or under 13. If they score exactly 13 both bets lose. Odds of even money are paid. If you are using a system for counting tens, you can use this information to your advantage and make this additional bet when the shoe is rich in tens.

Multiple action blackjack

In multiple action blackjack you keep the same hand for three games and the dealer keeps the same up card throughout. A poor hand may mean three losses but a good hand may lead to three wins.

6

PUNTO BANCO

Punto banco is a popular card game based on baccara. All winning bets are paid by the casino but the players take turns to control the bank. On average four decks of cards are used. Paddles are used to move the cards around.

Using a maximum of three cards, the players try to make a score as close as possible to 9.

Tens and court cards (kings, queens, jacks) have a value of 0.

Aces count as 1.

Cards 2 to 9 have their face value.

Scoring

The values of the cards are added to give the score. Cards with a joint total of 10 are given a value of 0.

Examples
7 + 3 = 10 score = 0
8 + 2 = 10 score = 0
6 + 4 = 10 score = 0

Where the cards total more than 10, only the last figure of the total is counted as the score.

Examples
8 + 6 = 14 score = 4
10 + 9 = 19 score = 9, known as a 'natural'

The deal

The cards are shuffled and placed in a shoe. A blank card is inserted about one pack from the end to indicate when the cards should be re-shuffled.

Each player makes a bet. The players and the banker each receive two cards. The dealer announces the totals of each hand. If the totals are 8 or 9 that is a 'natural' and no further cards are dealt.

There are set rules which determine whether or not a third card should be dealt.

Chart detailing when an extra card is drawn on punto banco

Player having		
1 2 3 4 5 0	draws a card	
6 7	stands	
8 9	natural banker cannot draw	

Banker having	draws when giving	stands when player's third card is:
3	1 2 3 4 5 6 7 8 9 0	8
4	2 3 4 5 6 7	1 8 9 0
5	4 5 6 7	1 2 3 8 9 0
6	6 7	1 2 3 4 5 8 9 0
7	stands	
8 9	natural player cannot draw	

Betting

Each player is playing against the bank and not against one another. The hand with a score closest to the 9 wins. The bets are either 'banco' for the bank's hand to win or 'punto' for the player's hand to win. In some casinos it is also possible to bet on a tie.

The layout of tables varies but they are clearly marked with boxes where the banco and the punto bets should be placed.

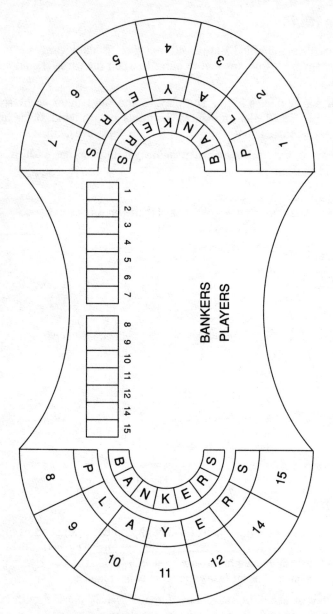

Figure 6.1 The betting layout for punto banco

The odds

Punto bets are paid at evens.

Banco bets are paid at 19/20 (evens less 5 per cent commission).

How to play

Two cards are alternately dealt to the punto and the banco hands. Where the first two cards total 8 or 9 this is known as a 'natural' and wins outright without the need to take further cards. When there is a

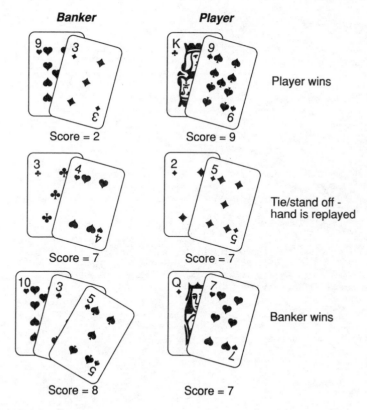

Figure 6.2 Punto banco hands

tie the hand is replayed. A total of 0 is the worst hand and is known as 'baccara'. The person holding the bank will continue to do so until the banker's hand loses. The bank is then passed to the right, but if the player wishes it can be passed earlier.

The players do not need to make any decisions, so they cannot influence the outcome. The only way a player can influence his winnings is through his betting strategy – betting higher stakes when on a winning run and reducing stakes or leaving the table when he starts losing.

The systems described for betting on the even chance bets on roulette can also be applied to punto banco. These include the martingale and the labouchere.

7
DICE AND COIN GAMES

Dice/craps

Dice is an exciting and extremely noisy game with lots of shouting and cheering. The complex betting layout makes it appear more difficult than it actually is. The basic game is relatively easy to learn. Although the layout incorporates a wide choice of bets, in practice only a few are worth playing.

Players take turns to throw two, six-sided dice the length of the table/pit. The dice must be thrown together and must hit the wall at the opposite end of the table. To calculate the score the number of spots on the uppermost faces are added. See Figure 7.1 for examples.

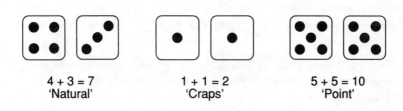

4 + 3 = 7
'Natural'

1 + 1 = 2
'Craps'

5 + 5 = 10
'Point'

Figure 7.1 Dice scores

The object of the game

Players predict whether or not the shooter (the person who throws the dice) will throw a winning or a losing score.

The first throw of the dice is called the 'come out roll'. A first throw of 7 or 11 is a winning score. A throw of 2, 3 or 12 is a losing score (craps). Any other score (4, 5, 6, 8, 9 or 10) means that a point is established. When a point is established, the player will try to make the point by re-throwing the dice any number of times to repeat the original score. If the original score is thrown before a 7 or 11, it is a winning score. If a 7 or 11 is thrown first, it is a losing score.

How to play

When it is your turn to be the shooter (the one who throws the dice) you must place a bet on win pass or don't pass (win or don't win). You continue to throw until there is a losing decision (a miss out).

The first throw is called the come out. If a 7 or 11 is thrown the bet on the pass (win) lines wins (a winning decision) and the bet on don't pass loses. If 2, 3, or 12 (craps) is thrown the bet on the pass line loses (a losing decision) and the bet on the don't pass line wins.

If a point is established (a score of 4, 5, 6, 8, 9 or 10), the shooter continues rolling the dice. If the point is made (the original score re-thrown) the pass bet wins and the don't pass bet loses. If a 7 or 11 is thrown the don't pass bet wins and the pass bet loses.

Types of bets

There is a wide range of bets. Try to familiarise yourself with them and learn where they are placed on the layout before you play (see Figure 7.2).

Pass (win) line

Win bets must be placed before the come out roll. They cannot be removed or reduced after the point is established. It wins if a 7 or 11 is

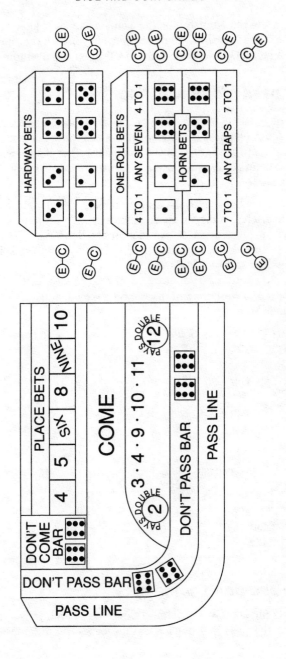

Figure 7.2 The betting layout for dice

thrown on the come out roll or if a point is made. It loses if craps (a score of 2, 3 or 12) is thrown on the come out roll or if the shooter fails to make a point. Odds of even money (1/1) are paid on winning bets.

Don't pass (don't win) line

This is the opposite of pass. The bet must be placed before the come out roll. After a point is established it can be reduced or removed. The bet wins if craps is thrown on the come out roll or if the shooter fails to make a point. It loses if 7 or 11 is thrown on the come out roll or if a point is made.

A lot of casinos bar one of the craps numbers, usually either 12 or 2, to give themselves a bigger house advantage. If a score is barred it is shown by an illustration of two dice in the don't win section – two ones if 2 is barred and two sixes if 12 is barred. If a score is barred it is void (neither wins nor loses).

The effect of a sequence of throws on the pass and don't pass bets

	Throw	Score	Pass bet	Don't pass bet	
Example 1	1st	7	wins	loses	
Example 2	1st	6*			
	2nd	5			
	3rd	5			
	4th	2			
	5th	6**	wins	loses	
Example 3	1st	6*			
	2nd	5			
	3rd	4			
	4th	7**	loses	wins	
Example 4	1st		3 (craps)	loses	wins
* point established					
** point made					

Come and don't come bets

These bets allow players who miss the come out roll to bet. They are similar to the pass and don't pass line bets. The difference is that they can be placed on any throw of the dice after the come out roll. When the bet is placed, the next throw of the dice becomes the first throw for the bet.

The rules concerning the win/loss are the same as the pass line. If a 7 or 11 is thrown the come bets win and don't come bets lose. If craps is thrown the come bets lose and the don't come bets win. Any other number thrown establishes a point. If the point is made the come bets win and don't come bets lose. However, the score need not be the same as for the pass bets. Scores of 2 or 12 may be barred for don't come bets (see section on don't pass bets).

If, for example, a come bet was placed on the third throw and the score is 6, the come bet will win if another score of 6 is thrown before a 7 or 11.

When a come or don't come bet is placed, the dealer will move the bet to the box of the score required. Come bets cannot be reduced or removed after a point is established. Don't come bets may be removed or reduced after a point is established.

Odds bets

These are additional bets which can be made once a point has been established. You must already have a bet on pass, don't pass, come or don't come. The bets are paid out at the true mathematical odds and are worth playing as the house advantage is reduced. However, casinos limit the amount that you can bet. Some allow a bet of up to the amount of your original wager, others allow you to bet double the original wager. Odds bets can be reduced or removed at anytime.

On the come out roll, come odds bets are 'off' but may be called 'on' by the player and don't come odds bets are 'on'.

Place bet

This is a bet on the individual scores of 4, 5, 6, 8, 9 or 10. It wins if the score selected is thrown before a 7 is rolled. These bets can be made at any time. They are placed by the dealer. You simply call out the bet you want and pass across the necessary chips. Place bets are 'off' at the come out roll unless you call them 'on'. The bets can be increased, decreased, removed or called off at any time.

Buy bet

Buy bets are similar to place bets except that a 5 per cent commission is paid when the bet is placed. The bets are then settled at the true mathematical odds. An easy way to find 5 per cent is to halve the amount of your bet and move the decimal point one place to the left. If you have any difficulty calculating the commission, simply ask the dealer to work it out for you. These bets are also placed by the dealer who will place a buy button on top of your chips. Always pay attention to ensure the dealer is placing your bets correctly to avoid disputes.

The bets may be increased, decreased or removed at any time and the commission adjusted accordingly each time.

If your buy bet wins and you leave it on again, you need to pay an additional 5 per cent commission. Buy bets are automatically 'off' on the come out roll, but may be called 'on' by the player.

Lay bets

Lay bets are the opposite of buy bets. If a 7 is rolled before the number on which a lay bet is wagered, the wager wins at true odds. The wager loses if the number on which a lay bet is wagered rolls before a 7 is rolled.

For a lay bet, the 5 per cent commission is charged on the amount the wager could win (not on the amount wagered as with buy bets). So, if you place a £40 bet on 4, the winnings would be £20 (£20 at 1/2 = £60, £60 – £40 stake = £20). Commission payable is 5 per cent of £20 = £1. You would therefore need to give the dealer £41. If you have any difficulty working out the commission, ask the dealer how much you need to pay.

One roll bets

Some bets are made on just one roll of the dice.

Field – for the numbers 2, 3, 4, 9, 10, 11 or 12 to be thrown. It loses if a 5, 6, 7 or 8 is rolled.

Hardways – throwing the same number on each dice. Hardway four is two deuces, hardway six is two threes, hardway eight is two fours and hardway ten is two fives. A hardway bet is for the numbers 4, 6, 8 or 10 to be rolled hardway. Hardways are 'off' on the come out roll but can be called 'on'.

Any seven – for a 7 to be rolled.

Any craps – the numbers 2, 3 or 12.

Craps two – number 2 (two ones).

Craps twelve – a bet on number 12 (two sixes).

Craps three – number 3 (a 2 and a 1).

Eleven – number 11 (5 and 6).

Horn – the bet is made in units of four. It is for the numbers 2, 3, 11 or 12 being rolled. It is treated as four separate bets on each number.

Horn high – the same as a horn bet except that there is one stake unit on each of the numbers and an extra stake unit on any of the numbers that the player nominates. So if number 11 was nominated it would have two stake units on it.

Dice payout odds and house advantage

Payout odds	House advantage per cent
Pass line 1/1 even	1.41
Don't pass line 1/1 even	1.4–4.38 depending on numbers barred
Come 1/1 even	1.41
Don't come 1/1 even	1.4–4.38 depending on numbers barred
Odds pass line and come	
4 or 10 2/1 (1/2)*	0
5 or 9 3/2 (2/3)*	0
6 or 8 6/5 (5/6)*	0
* Odds don't pass line and don't come	
Place bets (to win)	
4 or 10 9/5	6.7
5 or 9 7/5	4
6 or 8 7/6	1.5

Payout odds		House advantage per cent
Buy bets		
4 or 10 2/1		5
5 or 9 3/2		5
6 or 8 6/5		5
Lay bets		
4 or 10 1/2		2.5
5 or 9 2/3		3.2
6 or 8 5/6		4
Field (one roll bet)		
3, 4, 9, 10, 11 1/1		11.11
2 or 12 2/1		5.55
Hardways		
4 or 10 7/1		11.1
6 or 8 9/1		9.09
One roll bets		
Any seven	4/1	16.67
Any craps (2, 3 or 12)	7/1	11
Craps two	30/1	14
Craps three	15/1	11
Craps twelve	30/1	14
Eleven	15/1	11

— Chances of throwing each score —

There are 36 different ways in which the dice can be thrown. A score of 7 can be made in six different ways and a score of 11 can be made two ways. A point can be established in 24 different ways. There is only one way each of throwing 2 or 12 and two ways to throw 3. Therefore, you stand a fairly good chance of either throwing a natural or establishing a point on the come out roll.

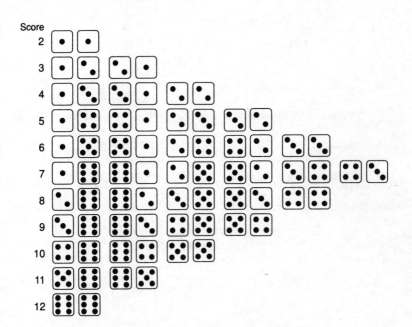

Figure 7.3 The different ways of making scores

Chances of throwing each score

2	2.77%
3	5.55%
4	8.33%
5	11.11%
6	13.88%
7	16.66%
8	13.88%
9	11.11%
10	8.33%
11	5.55%
12	2.77%

Chances of throwing each score on the come out roll

Natural 7 or 11	22.22% (8/36)
Point 4, 5, 6, 8, 9, 10	66.66% (24/36)
Craps 2, 3 or 12	11.11% (4/36)

Once a point has been made the chances of making it are as follows

4	8.33%
5	11.11%
6	13.88%
8	13.88%
9	11.11%
10	8.33%

House advantage

The house advantage for bets on the pass line is 1.41 per cent. For the don't pass line the advantage varies depending on how many numbers are barred. Where no numbers are barred the house advantage is 1.402 per cent but can be as high as 4.38 per cent if three numbers are barred. To give yourself the best advantage, you should try to play on tables where no numbers are barred, or at worst, only one.

Can the shooter influence the numbers the dice will land on?

It is difficult to influence the numbers that the dice will land on because the wall of the dice table is covered in small pyramids. As the dice hit the wall they are turned at different angles. This makes it virtually impossible to predict what number will be thrown.

——— Playing strategies ———

The best value bets are the pass, don't pass, come and don't come bets. They also allow the player to make odds bets. By taking advantage of the odds bets you can cut the house advantage to less than one per cent.

Playing these bets is the easiest way to win. However, the gains on each bet are small and it can take a long time to accumulate a significant amount. It is for this reason that many players risk their money on the bets with bigger odds, even though the house advantage is higher.

Systems

Many of the systems developed for playing the even money chances on roulette can be adapted and used to bet on the pass, don't pass, come and don't come bets (see the section on roulette).

The win and lose system (insurance system)

There are lots of variations on this system. Two bets are made, one on the don't pass line and if a point is established a place bet is made. If the point is not made, the don't pass line bet wins but the place bet loses, and vice versa if the point is made.

The system relies on the fact that you lose only if 7 or 11 is thrown on the come out roll. There are eight chances in 36 that you will lose – 22.22 per cent. This is outweighed by a 77.78 per cent chance of either winning or breaking even.

The advantage of this system is that it keeps losses to a minimum. The disadvantage is that winnings can take a long time to accumulate.

Example
If you bet £1 on don't pass and the first number thrown is 4, you then put a place bet on 4 of £1.

Total stakes = £2.

If 7 or 11 is thrown on the come out roll you lose £1.

If craps is thrown on the come out roll returns are £2.

If a point is made returns are £2.80

If the point is not made returns are £2.00

You win money if the point is made and break even if it is not. If you lose, only half of your total stake is lost.

Two-up/Pitch and toss

Two up is extremely popular in Australia. Traditionally played on Anzac Day, it is derived from the old British game of pitch and toss – a simple coin tossing game. Like dice, the game is very noisy with lots of shouting.

The object of the game is to predict how two coins, traditionally pennies, will land after being tossed into the air. Players bet on whether there will be two heads or two tails. A head and a tail (odds) is usually a tie. Winning bets are usually paid at even money.

There are four possible outcomes with coins A and B:

A – heads   B – heads
A – tails   B – tails
A – heads   B – tails
A – tails   B – heads

The game is played in a pit, and the two coins are placed on to a short piece of wood called a kip and tossed into the air by the spinner. Each player takes a turn at being the spinner. The spinner must state whether he is going for heads or tails.

Even money is paid for both two heads and two tails. If 'odds' is thrown, all bets are frozen. A side bet can be placed on the spinner consecutively throwing three heads or three tails without an odds in between. This bet is paid at 7.5/1. All bets lose if five consecutive odds are thrown. This gives the casino a house advantage of 3.12 per cent.

There is a 25 per cent chance that either two heads or two tails will be thrown and a 50 per cent chance for one head and one tail.

The systems recommended for betting on the even chances in roulette can be used as they will ensure that losses are minimised.

8
POKER

What is poker?

The term poker is used for a wide range of card games that are based on the ranking of five card hands. The object of the game is to win the money bet by having the best ranking hand. In order to win you need to beat all of your opponents. The casino supplies the dealer, charging a percentage of the pot (the money bet) for this service. A deduction of around 10 per cent is common.

The main attraction of poker is that it is a game of skill. With many card games you rely totally on the luck of the deal. Poker is entirely different. Even if you have the worst possible hand you can still win the game with the skilful use of bluffing. You fool the other players into thinking that you have a good hand.

The standard ranking of hands

The aim of poker is to win the pot by having the highest ranking hand. A poker hand is made up from five cards. The more difficult a hand is to achieve, the higher its position in the ranking. Figure 8.1 shows how the hands are ranked.

Each type of hand is also ranked according to the values of the cards. The highest value cards are aces and the lowest are twos. The cards are ranked in the following descending order: A,K,Q,J,10,9,8,7,6,5,4,3,2.

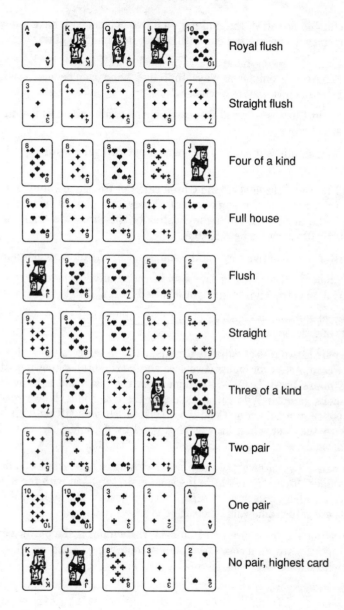

Figure 8.1 Poker hands ranked from highest to lowest

The suits do not affect the ranking, so if two players both have a royal flush, one with hearts and one with spades, the hands will tie.

The highest ranking hand is a royal flush – A,K,Q,J,10 in the same suit. There are only four ways that this hand can be made, with hearts, diamonds, spades or clubs.

A straight flush is a run of five cards of the same suit in consecutive numerical order.

Four of a kind is four cards of the same numerical value with any other card.

A full house is three of a kind (three cards of the same value) and a pair (two cards of the same value). Where two players have a full house, the hand with the highest value for the three of a kind wins. So 10,10,10,2,2 would beat 8,8,8,A,A.

A flush is a run of five cards of the same suit in any numerical order.

A straight is five cards of any suit in consecutive numerical order. A,K,Q,J,10 is the highest straight followed by K,Q,J,10,9.

Three of kind is three cards of the same numerical value with two cards of different values.

Two pair is two sets of pairs (two cards with the same value) with any other card. Aces over eights (two aces and two eights) is known as the dead man's hand. It takes its name from the last hand held by the infamous gambler Wild Bill Hickock. In the late 1800s, he was playing poker in a saloon at Deadwood, Dakota. He was sitting with his back to the door when he was shot dead by Jack McCall. His last hand consisted of a pair of aces and a pair of eights.

One pair is two cards of the same value with three other cards of different values. If two players have the same pair, the hand with the highest value other cards wins. A,A,10,7,5 would beat A,A,9,7,5. If all of the cards are of the same value then there is a tie.

Where none of the above hands is held, the winner is the player with the highest card. In a showdown a hand containing an ace would beat one with a king and so on.

The basic game

Poker is played with one deck of 52 cards with the jokers removed. Before any cards are dealt, players make an initial bet called an ante-bet. All the bets are placed in the centre of the table.

Each player receives five cards dealt face down. Players look at their cards and a round of betting commences starting with the player to the left of the dealer.

Each player has the option of betting or folding (withdrawing from the game). A player holding a poor hand may decide to fold. If you fold your cards they are returned to the dealer without being revealed to the other players. You lose any bets made.

Some games allow players to check. This usually happens on the first round of betting after the cards have been dealt. Players do not have to participate in the first round of betting, instead they announce 'check'. If they want to continue in the game they must bet on their next turn.

The first bet determines how much each player has to bet in order to stay in the game. Players may also raise the bet up to the agreed maximum. To stay in the game you need to bet at least as much as the previous player. Betting continues until either only one player remains or there is a showdown and players reveal their hands. If only one player remains (all the others having folded) he will win the pot. He does not reveal his cards to the other players. If there is a showdown, the player with the highest ranking poker hand wins the pot. In the event of a tie the pot is shared.

In Figure 8.2, player D would win in a showdown as he has the highest ranking hand.

This is poker in its simplest form but it is hardly ever played in this manner. Lots of variations have been introduced to make the games more exciting and challenging.

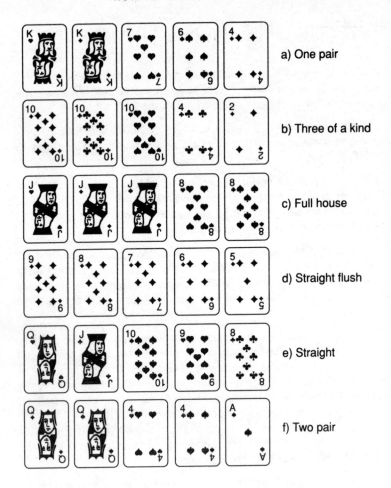

a) One pair

b) Three of a kind

c) Full house

d) Straight flush

e) Straight

f) Two pair

Figure 8.2 Example hands in poker

Understanding the odds

In order to play poker well a good understanding of the odds of being dealt particular hands is essential. With games like draw poker you need to know the chances of improving on your hand.

The likelihood of being dealt a particular hand in poker		
Hand dealt	*Number of ways it can be made*	*Odds against it being dealt in your first hand*
Royal flush	4	649,739/1
Straight flush	36	72,192/1
Four of a kind	624	4,164/1
Full house	3,744	693/1
Flush	5,108	508/1
Straight	10,200	254/1
Three of a kind	54,912	46/1
Two pair	123,552	20/1
One pair	1,098,240	15/11
Highest card	1,302,540	1/1

Stakes

The minimum stakes on many poker games are low. The higher the stakes, the better the players, so while you are still learning stick to the cheaper games and gradually work your way up.

The minimum amount of capital you need varies depending on the game. As a rough guide, the capital needed for a game of draw poker is around forty times the minimum stake. With seven card stud, approximately fifty times the minimum stake should be sufficient. Games like hold 'em and omaha need around one hundred times the minimum stake. By dividing the amount that you have budgeted for by the minimum capital required, you can find the minimum stakes that you can play for.

——— Strategies for success ———

Get plenty of practice

You need to be able to recognise the value of your hand and where it comes in the ranking immediately. Deal out hands of five cards, identify the poker hands and put them in the correct ranking order. Once you have mastered the ranking you can then start to judge whether or not a hand is worth playing.

Get plenty of practice. Take a pack of cards and deal out dummy hands as if you are playing the game with several players. Practise placing bets as you play. Look at your own hand. Decide whether or not it is worth playing. Then assess your hand against the others. Did you make a good decision? Would any of the other hands have beaten yours? Are you throwing away hands that could easily win? By continuing to do this you will learn the sorts of hands that are worthwhile playing and those that are not.

Body language

Poker relies on the other players not knowing your hand. Although the other players cannot see your hand, the way that you react to its contents can give them a lot of information.

Players who have complete control over their mannerisms make better poker players. If you can look at your cards without showing any facial expressions you make it impossible for the other players to glean any information about your hand.

Keep records

After each game write down the reasons why you won or lost. Analyse the results and learn from your mistakes.

If you lost, try to determine why. Were you staying in when you should have folded? Were you folding with hands that could have won? Were you failing to force other players into folding? Was your body language giving away information?

Carry out the same procedure when you win. Was it because your strategy was good? Were you just dealt lots of good hands? Did other players make stupid mistakes? Were you picking up on any signs given by the other players?

Periodically analyse your records. They will tell you if you're sticking to your budget and if your betting strategy is effective.

Vary your play

Try not to stick to one style of playing. The most successful poker players are those who are totally unpredictable. If you play cautiously in some hands and aggressively in others you will confuse the opposition. You should aim to vary your betting, the number of cards you take (if playing a draw game), how often you bluff and the signals that you give.

Developing a betting strategy

You need to develop a betting strategy that will maximise your winnings whilst minimising your losses. Your betting strategy also needs to be varied so that the other players can't predict what your hand is. If you always double the stakes when you have a good hand it will soon be noted by the other players. Just because your hand is poor it doesn't automatically mean you will lose. Having the nerve to bluff and back up the bluff with a heavy round of betting can cause other players to fold, even though their hands may be better than yours.

Throughout the game you need to pay attention to the way your opponents are playing. Some players may back down after a modest raise while others may need a huge raise in order to fold. You will be able to spot the players who are staying in the game simply because it is not costing them very much. You may notice that one particular player always folds early on when he has nothing. If he is still there in the later rounds of betting, you will know to treat him with caution.

It is also important to know when to fold. If your hand isn't good enough to win you should withdraw from the game. By continually staying in for one extra round of betting with a hand that is clearly going to get beaten, you lose more money than you need to.

9

TIPS FOR PLAYING POKER

Five card draw

Each player receives five cards face down and after an initial round of betting has the opportunity to exchange any card in his hand for new cards from the deck. It is usual to select the cards that are being discarded and to return them to the dealer before new cards are drawn.

Odds against improving hands in draw poker

Hand held	Cards drawn	Desired hand	Odds against achieving hand
Three of a kind	2	any improvement	17/2
Three of a kind + kicker	1	any improvement	11/1
Three of a kind	1	full house	15/1
Three of a kind	1	four of a kind	46/1
Three of a kind	2	full house	15/1
Three of a kind	2	four of a kind	23/1
Two pair	1	full house	11/1
Two pair	3	three of a kind	7.5/1
One pair	3	full house	97/1
One pair	3	four of a kind	359/1
One pair + kicker	2	any improvement	3/1
One pair + kicker	2	two pair using kicker	7.5/1

One pair + kicker	2	two pair without kicker	17/1
One pair + kicker	2	three of a kind	12/1
One pair + kicker	2	full house	119/1
One pair + kicker	2	fours	1080/1
Four card flush	1	pair	3/1
Four card flush	1	flush	4.5/1
Four card open ended	1	straight flush	2/1
Straight flush		straight flush	22.5/1
Incomplete straight	1	any improvement	1/1
Flush (inside)		pair	3/1
		flush	5/1
		straight	11/1
		straight flush	46/1

Playing strategy

There is a general rule which says that if you get nothing from the deal you should fold. It is my belief that if you do not get at least a high pair you should fold.

From the number of cards that each player exchanges you may have an indication of the type of hand held. If you are holding a pair you can improve your hand by exchanging up to three cards. However, if you exchange three cards, the other players will immediately be aware that you are likely to have a pair.

Anyone with two pair or three of a kind will be confident that he has a better hand.

Instead of drawing three cards, you have the option of keeping a kicker. The kicker will usually be your highest other card. Instead of exchanging three cards, you exchange two. Your chances of improving on your hand are slightly reduced but now the other players will be unsure as to whether you only have a pair or a possible three of a kind.

Do not fall into the pattern of always retaining a kicker when you have a pair as the other players will soon work out your strategy. Vary your play as much as possible so that your opponents are never sure about your hand.

Example game

Figure 9.1 shows the hands of four players before and after the draw.

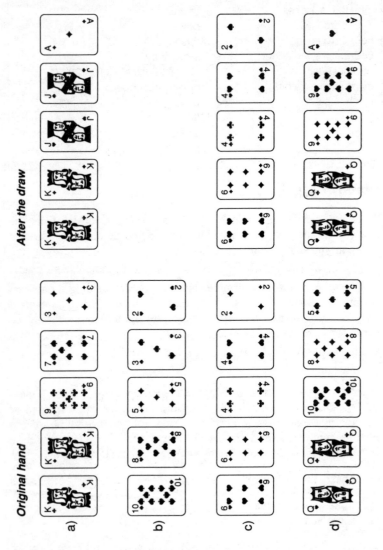

Figure 9.1 Example hands in draw poker

Player A is dealt a good initial hand with a pair of kings. Three cards are drawn. He fails to get three of a kind but gets another pair. The fifth card is an ace. He knows that even if another player has a pair of aces, the fact that he is holding an ace makes it harder for him to achieve three of a kind.

Player B has a poor initial hand so decides to fold.

Player C has two pair. Although the cards are low, he has the opportunity of making a full house by drawing one card. He has seen player A draw three cards, so he knows that A's initial hand is a pair. He fails to improve his hand.

Player D has a high pair of two queens. He is aware that A also initially had a pair. Player C only took one card so he is possibly going for a full house, a flush a straight or is bluffing. D draws three cards and improves to two pair.

Player A raises. Player C decides to fold – he realises that player A may have improved, possibly to three of a kind or two pair. Although player C has two pair, they are low value cards.

Player D knows he has a fairly good hand so he raises player A. He knows two pair with kings or aces could beat him. He holds an ace so knows the chances of player A holding a pair of aces or three aces is reduced.

The game now becomes a test of nerves between A and D. If either backs down then the other will win the pot. If the game continues to a showdown then player A will win the showdown.

Five card stud

Each player receives five cards from which they make their best five card poker hand. Initially each player is dealt one card face up and one face down. The player with the lowest face-up card must make a forced bet. The remaining cards are dealt face up. A round of betting takes place after each card is dealt. The player showing the highest ranking hand is the first to bet in each round.

Here you progressively get more information on which to base your decisions. Once all the cards have been dealt you should have a pretty good idea of your opponents' likely hands.

Strategy

If you cannot match or better the highest card showing you should fold. Ideally aim for a minimum hand of a high pair.

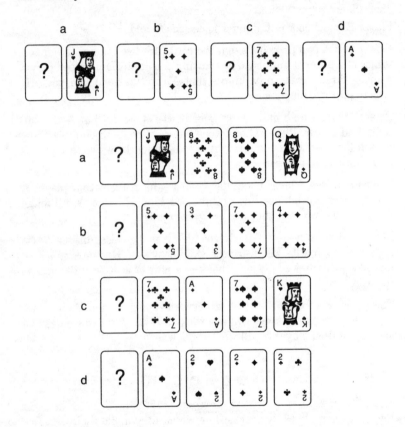

Figure 9.2 Example hands in five card stud poker

See Figure 9.2. In the initial deal, player B has the lowest face up card so makes a forced bet. As each card is dealt you get more information about each player's hand. By the fourth card players A, C and D are all showing pairs. Player B has the potential to achieve a straight flush.

By the time the fifth card has been dealt, you can clearly see what the possible hands are. The best hands are A – three of a kind with eights, B – a straight flush, C – three of a kind with sevens and D – four of a kind with twos. If each player has achieved his best possible hand then player B would win on a showdown.

Each player needs to assess his chances of winning against the other hands.

If player A has another 8, he is certain of beating player C. He also knows that if B has any card other than a diamond then his hand is worth nothing. If player D's hole card (the card dealt face down) is not a 6 or an ace then player A will also beat him. One of the aces is revealed in player C's hand, which gives D less chance of achieving a full house.

Player B knows that he has potentially the best hand. If his hole card is not a diamond then whether or not he wins will depend on how well he can bluff.

If player C has another 7, he will have to decide whether or not the other players are bluffing. Although all the players have the potential for good hands it is unlikely that they have all achieved them. If the other players are all bluffing then he would win a showdown.

If player D has either a 2 or an ace then the only danger is player B. To beat him player B would need to be holding the 6 of diamonds. Any other diamond would only give player B a flush. However, if player D is not holding another 2 or an ace, then he is in danger of being beaten by either A or B – both have the potential for a better three of a kind than his.

Seven card stud

Each player receives seven cards. The aim is to make the best possible five card poker hand from the seven cards dealt to you. The player with the best hand wins all the money staked less the rake.

Initially three cards are dealt, two face down and one face up. The fourth, fifth and sixth cards are dealt face up and the seventh face down. You therefore have four cards on display to the other players and three cards which are hidden from view.

There is a round of betting after each card has been dealt. The person with the highest ranking poker hand on view is the first to either bet or fold in each round of betting. So someone with three of a kind would be the first to bet if all the other players are showing one pair.

Here you have quite a lot of useful information on which to base your strategy. You may be able to deduce from the other players' cards on display that your hand has no chance of winning. You can use your knowledge of the odds to calculate your opponents' chances of completing hands that are shown. However, the other players can also deduce the same amount of information from your cards on view.

If your cards on display show the potential for a good hand that could beat the likely hands of all the other players but you do not hold the cards necessary, you have the option to bluff. By continually raising the stakes you may force the other players to fold.

Example hands

Figure 9.3 Example hands in seven card stud poker

See Figure 9.3. Suppose you are player A. You have two pair. You can immediately see that player B has a better hand with three of a kind. Player C also has two pair which beats your hand, but could have a full house if he has either another king or another 5. In the cards that you are showing, you have the 9, 8 and 7 of hearts. Although your hand can't win in a showdown against either A or B, by using a heavy round of betting you could convince them that you have the other two cards needed to complete the straight flush.

Hold 'em

Each player receives two cards face down. Five cards are then placed face up in the centre of the table. These cards are used by all the players. Each player uses any combination of the two cards in their hand and the five community cards to make the best five card poker hand.

The deal

Initially each player receives their two hidden cards followed by a round of betting. Players often have the opportunity to bet blind (to place a bet before they look at their cards) which helps to increase the pot. Three of the community cards are then dealt, called the flop. Another round of betting follows. A further community card is dealt followed by a round of betting and then the final community card is dealt.

Since each player's cards are hidden from view, the only indication you have of their possible hands are the way in which they are betting. In order to make a proper assessment, you really need to see all of the community cards first. Once you have seen these, you are then in a better position to assess the likely hands.

Strategy before the flop

You need to decide whether or not your two cards are worth playing. In general terms it is worthwhile playing any pair, consecutive cards of the same suit, such as 9,8 or 6,5 and fairly high cards of the same suit such as J,9.

Strategy after the flop

You now have a better indication of the possible hands. You can assess your position against all the other possibilities. It may be that the community cards do not help you and give other players the possibility of really good hands, in which case you should fold now.

If you are still in a fairly good position, you need to force out any-one who can beat you either now or once the other two cards have been dealt.

Nuts

Occasionally a situation may arise where you know that you have the best possible hand (nuts) that can be made using the community cards and that there is no way in which you can be beaten.

Example hands

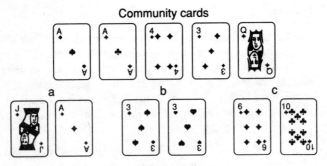

Figure 9.4 Example hands in hold 'em

See Figure 9.4. The best possible hand from the community cards is four of a kind, followed by a full house, then three of a kind.

Player A will deduce that he has a good hand with three of a kind. He knows that he has the best possible three of a kind and can only be beaten by a full house, and since he holds one of the aces, the chances of anyone holding either two queens, two fours or two threes are low.

However, player B has a full house. He knows that only four of a kind or a full house with queens or fours could beat him.

Player C has nothing and would be wise to fold. Betting would then commence between A and B. It will probably develop into a test of nerves to determine who will fold, or would ultimately lead to a show-down, which B would win.

Omaha

Each player receives four cards face down. Five cards are placed face up in the centre of the table to be used by all the players. Using any combination of two cards in your hand and three community cards, you make the best five card poker hand.

The game is dealt in a similar way to hold 'em with a flop of three cards. You may also be given the opportunity to bet blind (bet before looking at your cards). What makes the game more complicated is the way in which the five card poker hand is made. When you see the cards you need to give some thought as to what hand you have actually got. At first glance you may seem to have an exceptionally good hand, but you need to remember that you can only use two of the cards in your hand.

Community cards

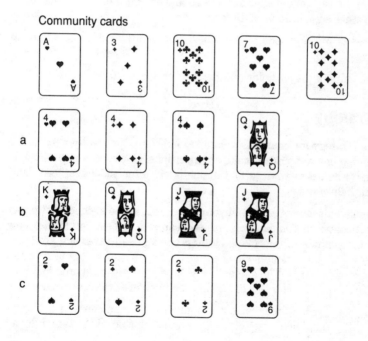

Figure 9.5 Example hands in omaha

See Figure 9.5. By looking at the cards in total, player A can immediately see a full house (three fours and two tens). However, because only two cards can be used from his hand he only has two pair (two tens and two fours).

Player B appears to have a straight (A, K, Q, J, 10) but the hand actually held is two pair (two jacks and two tens).

At first glance player C may appear to have a full house (three twos and two tens). However, he can only use two cards from his hand so only holds two pairs (two tens and two twos).

From the community cards, you can get a lot of information about the possible hands held by other players. In Figure 9.5, for example, the possible hands are:

Four of a kind – one player has the other two tens.

A full house – one player has one 10 and an ace, 7 or 3 or holds two of the other aces, sevens or threes.

Three of a kind – one of the other tens, or a pair of aces, sevens or threes.

Two pair – a player holds another pair or one ace, 7 or 2.

Strategy

The strategy for omaha is similar to hold 'em. You really need to see the flop before you can make any decisions. However, a situation can arise when it is wise to fold immediately after you have been dealt your hole cards.

Being dealt four of a kind in your hole cards is one of the worst possible situations. You can only use two cards so at best you have a pair with no chance of improving on them. Being dealt three of a kind also gives you only a remote chance that the fourth card will appear in the community cards. The same is true of being dealt four cards to a possible flush; your chances of making the flush are drastically reduced.

The best cards to play with are high pairs or high cards of the same suit (if you hold only two of the same suit) which could lead to a flush.

After the flop, you are in a much better position to judge your chances of winning. You can then assess all of the possibilities and work out

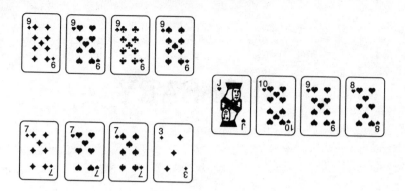

Figure 9.6 Hands to fold on in omaha

your chances of making a good hand. It is at this stage that you need to force out any players who have the potential to improve their hands into ones that could beat yours.

Nuts

As with hold 'em, occasionally a situation may arise where you know that you have the best possible hand (nuts) that can be made using the community cards and that there is no way in which you can be beaten.

GLOSSARY

Active – bets that are on
Ante – a bet made before any cards dealt
Blind bet – a bet that is made without looking at your cards
Bluff – tricking the other players into thinking that you have a really good hand
Board – the community cards in games such as hold 'em and omaha
Boxcars – a score of 12 in dice
Bullet – an ace
Burnt card – a card that is removed from the pack and not used in play; often several of the top cards will be removed before hands are dealt to combat cheating by the dealer
Bust – a score over 21 in blackjack
Button – a plastic marker used in casino games to denote an imaginery dealer which ensures that no player gains an advantage from his position relative to the actual dealer
Cage – cash point where chips are exchanged for money
Call – a verbal statement that a player will match the previous bet
Card counting – a system of counting cards which tips the odds in the player's favour
Car jockey – someone employed by the casino to park the customers' cars
Chip – a plastic disc used in place of money for betting
Community cards – cards that can be used by all the players to make up their best five card poker hand in games such as hold 'em and omaha
Commission – a charge made by the casino for the use of its facilities, usually a percentage of the pot

Croupier – dealer
Dead man's hand – two pair of aces over eights
Deuce – two
Door card – in stud poker, the first card that is dealt face up
Draw – exchanging cards in your hand for cards from the deck
Flop – the deal where the first three community cards are revealed in hold 'em and omaha
Flush – five cards of the same suit
Fold – withdraw from the game
Fours – four cards of the same value, for example, four queens
Full house – three cards of the same value with a pair, for example, three aces and two sixes
Hit – draw another card
Hole cards – the players' cards that are dealt face down
Impair – odd numbers on roulette
Inactive – bets are are 'off' in dice
Kicker – in draw poker, a card retained to make it more difficult for your opponents to guess your hand
Little Joe – a score of four in dice
Manque – the lower numbers 1–18 in roulette
Marked cards – cards that have been marked in some way so that a cheat can identify their values from looking at the backs of the cards
Natural – a 7 or 11 on the first throw in dice
Neighbours – adjacent numbers on a roulette wheel
Ninety days – a score of 9 in dice
Nuts – having a hand in games such as hold 'em and omaha which is the best possible hand and one which cannot be beaten by any other player
Pair – the even numbers on roulette
Passe – the high numbers 19–36 on roulette
Plaque – a square chip, usually of a high denomination
Pocket cards – cards which are dealt face down in hold 'em and omaha
Poker face – having complete control over your facial expressions so that you do not give your opponents any clues about your hand
Pot – the money bet in poker that is placed in the centre of the table
Rake – in poker, a charge made by the casino for the use of its facilities, usually a percentage of the pot
River – the last round of betting in poker
Run – another name for a straight
See – the same as 'call'

Shoe or **sabot** – a box where cards are placed for dealing
Showdown – when the players reveal their hands in poker
Snake eyes – a score of 2 in dice
Stake – the amount of money bet
Straight – five cards of any suit in consecutive order
Street – a round of betting – first street is the first round of betting, second street the second and so on
Stud – a form of poker where some cards are dealt face up
Sweeten – to add money to the pot, usually in the form of an ante bet
Technician – someone who is skilled at manipulating the cards so that he can deal himself a good hand
Threes – three cards of the same value
Trips – three cards of the same value
Vigorish – commission

APPENDIX

Gamblers Anonymous organisations — in Great Britain, the United States — and Australia

Great Britain
Gamblers Anonymous
National Service Office
PO Box 88
London
SW10 0EU
Telephone: 0171 384 3040

United States
Gamblers Intergroup
PO Box 7
New York
New York
10116
Telephone : (212) 265 8600

Australia
Gamblers Anonymous
Head Office
Corner of Dorcas and
   Montague Street
South Melbourne
Telephone: (3) 696 6108

Gamblers Anonymous
PO Box Burwood
Sydney
NSW 2134
Telephone: (02) 564 1574

INDEX

ty TEACH YOURSELF

SUCCESSFUL GAMBLING

Belinda Levez

Teach Yourself Successful Gambling is a complete guide to gambling and betting.

Belinda Levez is a former betting shop manager and casino croupier. In this book she shares her inside knowledge, to help you maximise your winnings. All the main areas of gambling are covered:

- racing
- sports
- casino games
- lotteries
- bingo
- pools
- slot machines

This book will be a real help both for those who know nothing about gambling and betting and for those with some experience who want to learn more and improve the odds for success.